For You

Inspired Messages

Yvette Lynn Burrel Jackson

BK
ROYSTON
Publishing

BK Royston Publishing
P. O. Box 4321 | Jeffersonville, IN 47131
www.bkroystonpublishing.com

Copyright 2018

ISBN: 978-1-946111-59-3

Printed in the U.S.A.

DEDICATION

I dedicate this book to my three dear children Amber, Whitney and Austin who have been there for me through some of the hardest struggles of my life. The strength you exhibited for me when I was at some of my lowest points will not be forgotten. I am so thankful for the loyal and loving support you all have shown to me. I don't believe that I would be as focused and driven if you were not a part of my life.

You all inspire me to be a better parent, listener and friend. I am so proud of your accomplishments in life thus far and how you have beaten the odds that were stacked against you coming from a broken home.

You exemplify encouragement to your peers, friends and family even when you are facing your own problems. God blessed me with three beautiful, kind hearted and thoughtful children and a grandson Britain who is smart and handsome. I am grateful to be your mother and G G. I love you Amber, Whitney, Austin and Britain you inspire me to motivate others.

For You
Inspired Messages

Y L B

Acknowledgements

I want to acknowledge and thank my dear mother, Dr. Willi Burrel and father, Bishop William Burrel who has made his heavenly transition, for always believing in me and encouraging me to never give up even in the toughest situations. You are my inspiration and I have learned how to inspire others because of your examples. I am thankful to God and so proud to have such renowned parents that have motivated and mentored people all over the world through ministry.

I Love you mom and dad.

For You
Inspired Messages

Y L B

Table of Contents

WORDS FROM MY HEART

Life is full of ups and downs and all types of positive as well as negative occurrences. Just remember that you are not your experience, but if you learn from it, you will be better because of it. I know what it's like to struggle with fear, abuse, depression, divorce, joblessness, rejection, and loneliness. Maybe you have suffered some of the same hurdles in your life or are facing some uncomfortable issues at this time.

Instead of allowing the things that disappoint me get the best of me, I learned from them and through prayer and healing I can now inspire others by the grace of God. I am an over comer having gone through two very painful divorces that left me devastated and took a tremendous toll on my health. I have suffered two near death experiences in which I was hospitalized for 10 days in one case and almost a week in the other circumstance. Even with all of the discomfort I went through, I am able to say a kind word to those in need, and give a helping hand to those that are struggling. I am a survivor and so are you if you are reading this book. I couldn't do anything without my Lord and Savior Jesus Christ; he is my anchor and constant companion.

Every person has a story to tell of the obstacles they have faced and how they were able to endure and triumph. Trials of life can hit you blind-sided and cause you to lose focus on the gifts, talents and greatness born inside of you. When you are knocked down, get back up, when a door closes, don't fret, because God will open another door with greater rewards. I am not all the things I have been through and neither are you, by the mercies of God.

We can use the trials that we encountered as tools to relate to those that are going through similar life oppositions. We all have a purpose to fulfill that will impact someone else's life decisions. When we learn to leave the past out of the present, we will be more than a conqueror in the future. I hope these words from my heart help you to lift up, stand up and live up to the full potential that God has placed inside of you.

Blessings as you read.

INTRODUCTION

This book is full of great lessons to help educate and promote Spiritual and self-awareness to women, men and for mentoring youth groups. It is written in full color pages to grab the eyes of the reader and to bring motivation, inspiration and joy to all that read it. Our creator is the master of all colors within our universe. Colors are a gift from heaven displayed in the sky, earth, birds, fish, animals, elements, and even the human race has unique shades. Man can only try to duplicate the hues that God has originated through creation. A certain tint can change a person's mood. Colors do have an effect on people and that is why I believe I was inspired to write this book in decorated pages. I was moved by God to make each folio unique in graphics and dynamics so that the youth and adults could memorize the scriptures and messages. The page designs will help you gain a greater knowledge of the things pertaining to the bible and also everyday life.

The purpose is to teach you the reader through my short messages ways to stay encouraged, and learn to speak positive things into the atmosphere that will produce changes you desire. I am a former instructor of the Western

Michigan Bible Institute, I taught for a little over 5 years. Having knowledge of the names and attributes of God, I felt impressed by the Holy Spirit to include them in this book along with their definitions. It is my hope that something will be conveyed that will generate your ambition to pursue your hearts goals.

Writing this book is a part of my purpose and I am simply being obedient to the charge given to me to uplift, renew, motivate, encourage and inspire the readers. I sincerely hope that you enjoy *For You* Inspired Messages and are rejuvenated by the comforting quotes, scriptures, and messages contained within.

Chapter One

Quotes and
Inspired Messages

For You
Inspired Messages

Y L B

Yvette Lynn Burrel

TODAY

TODAY I will be the best person that I choose to be, because I decide to be happy or sad, and I choose happiness and well being. **TODAY** I will choose to forgive, over and over again because that is what it takes to press toward perfection. **TODAY** I will not hold onto grudges, because that will hold me back from moving forward into my future. **TODAY** I will think positive and speak abundance into my life. **TODAY** I will expect great things to happen for me, and to me. **TODAY** I will succeed in my endeavors when I put forth the right effort. **TODAY** I will not focus on negative circumstances in my life, because that will restrain my progress. **TODAY** I will be free in my inner spirit to love and be loved in return.

Yvette Lynn Burrel

LOVE

LOVE is freely given and willingly received when confidence and reliance have been achieved. LOVE is like medicine and helps to heal the wounded, so show love and someone close to you will become whole today.

1st John chapter 4 verse 16
[NLT]

We know how much God loves us, and we have put our trust in his love. God is love, and all who live in love live in God, and God lives in them.

Yvette Lynn Burrel

YESTERDAY

YESTERDAY'S hurt, rejection, disappointments, and failures are gone and will not dominate my thoughts for today. I choose to live in the present with expectations, and not to reside within yesterday's unanswered dreams. Letting go of yesterday's rejection will help to start a healing process for me today. YESTERDAY'S disappointments will help me to strive harder so that I won't make the same mistakes over and over. I choose to focus on today's new opportunities and embrace life rather than dwell on yesterday's regrets. YESTERDAY'S failure's have no power over today's triumph's, because everyday is a new beginning for greatness. YESTERDAY has its place, and it is to teach us that we can be better with each new day we are given, if we learn from our yesterday.

Yvette Lynn Burrel

STAYING STRONG

STAYING STRONG does not mean you won't have to shed some tears now and again. Your tears are not a sign of weakness, they will become healing and strength with every drop. STAYING STRONG means you are able to fully trust God who will help you get back up even if it takes days, weeks, months, and even years. Yes, he is your anchor and you are STAYING STRONG.

Yvette Lynn Burrel

HOPE

HOPE gives me expectation for things that I can not see at this present moment; therefore I will continue to hope for them. HOPE gives me energy to get up every morning and pursue my goals everyday. HOPE is a gift that is freely given to anyone that will embrace the power of positive thinking. HOPE makes the dark clouds of grief, sorrow, and depression disperse. I have the ability to create my own destiny when I hope for a better life. HOPE will defeat, doubt, hate, and violence, because hope embodies fortitude, courage and love. I can trust hope, because it has the strength and resilience I need to conquer all my fears. When I embrace hope, it gives me a sense of peace and calm. My life would lack bravery, if I did not allow hope to walk this journey with me. HOPE is my life line and will keep me a float, when my dreams are delayed.

Yvette Lynn Burrel

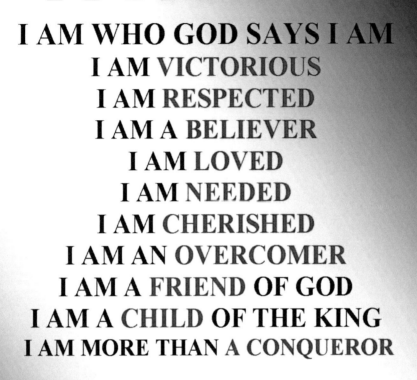

I AM WHO GOD SAYS I AM
I AM VICTORIOUS
I AM RESPECTED
I AM A BELIEVER
I AM LOVED
I AM NEEDED
I AM CHERISHED
I AM AN OVERCOMER
I AM A FRIEND OF GOD
I AM A CHILD OF THE KING
I AM MORE THAN A CONQUEROR

Yvette Lynn Burrel

BEAUTIFUL

Every person is BEAUTIFUL in
the eyes of another individual.
BEAUTIFUL is the reflection I see
each morning when I look into the
mirror. Flaws and all, nothing
superficial; BEAUTIFUL is still
who I am. God made everything
about me unique and special. I
am exactly how I should be
this very moment BEAUTIFUL.

Psalm 139 verse 14
[NLT]

Thank you for making me so
wonderfully complex! Your
workmanship is marvelous,
how well I know it.

Yvette Lynn Burrel

WORTH

WORTH says I am beautiful just the way I am, even with my imperfections. The worth of an individual should not be based upon other people's misguided opinions when looking at the outward appearance. **WORTH** will drive me away from someone that mistreats me, because I value myself much more than that. When I struggle with self worth, I can raise it up by loving myself, respecting myself & believing in myself. **WORTH** gives me boldness to hold my head up high, even when a person is trying to put me down low. Look in the mirror & realize your own unique beauty that no one else can duplicate & your self worth will begin to flourish. You're **WORTH** more than gold.

Yvette Lynn Burrel

SUCCESS

SUCCESS is mixed with both triumphs and failures. Those that achieve it are meticulous as well as driven. They will chase intently and wait expectedly to obtain SUCCESS.

Psalm 75 verses 6 & 7
[KJV]

[6] For promotion cometh neither from the east, nor from the west, nor from the south. [7] But God is the judge: He putteth down one, and setteth up another.

Yvette Lynn Burrel

Sometimes You Just Have To Wait,

PERFECTION

Takes Time.

GOD IS STILL WORKING ON ME.

Psalm 138 verse 8
[KJV]

The LORD will perfect that which concerneth me: thy mercy, O LORD, endureth for ever: forsake not the works of thine own hands.

Yvette Lynn Burrel

FRIENDSHIP

FRIENDSHIP is a bond accomplished after trust and kindheartedness has been demonstrated by each Individual. A friend is there in good times and they won't disappear when you go through a struggle.

Proverbs chapter 17 verse 17
[NLT]

A friend is always loyal, and a brother is born to help in time of need.

Yvette Lynn Burrel

HONESTY

HONESTY will open
the door for great
relationships to blossom
into lasting unions. Being
truthful will promote
feelings of self assurance,
and cancel thoughts
of mistrust.

Proverbs chapter 24 verse 26

An honest answer is
like a kiss on the lips.

Yvette Lynn Burrel

BELIEVE

BELIEVE that there is something greater waiting for you to acquire; then research and pursue it with diligence until it becomes yours.

1st John chapter 5 verse 13
[NIV]

I write these things to you who BELIEVE in the name of the Son of GOD so that you may know that you have eternal life.

Yvette Lynn Burrel

EMBRACE

EMBRACE the things
in life that really matter,
family, relationships, and
friendships. EMBRACE
change when you know
it is necessary for your
growth. EMBRACE the
fact that sometimes you
will make mistakes and
learn to get over them.
EMBRACE the challenge
if it will improve
your abilities.

Yvette Lynn Burrel

HAPPINESS

HAPPINESS is a state of
mind. It is not measured
by the money I possess.
Delight comes when
I know I've done my
best. **HAPPINESS** begins
with me and then it
will spread to others.

John chapter 15 verse 11
[NIV]
I have told you this so that
My Joy may be in you and
that your joy may be complete.

Yvette Lynn Burrel

COMMITMENTS

COMMITMENTS should never be taken lightly; because once you make a promise to someone it could be a life changing moment in their life. When you are committed you won't allow other things to distract you from fulfilling your mission. COMMITMENTS in relationships come from maturity, trust, honesty and love which cast out all fears and doubts. COMMITMENTS that are broken cause heart break and dysfunction. It is better not to commit, than to pledge and go back on your word. COMMITMENTS to finish what you have started are wise choices. COMMITMENTS are oaths of assurance that you will hold to your spoken word.

Yvette Lynn Burrel

NEVER GIVE UP

NEVER GIVE IN

NEVER TURN BACK

YOU'RE MADE FOR

GREATNESS

Yvette Lynn Burrel

MOTIVATION

MOTIVATION will keep me moving towards my dreams and goals with tenacity. It does not matter what obstacles I may encounter, as long as I have inspiration, my hopes will be manifested in time.

Romans chapter 8 verse 24
[ESV]
For in this hope we were saved. Now hope that is seen is not hope. For who hopes for what he sees?

Yvette Lynn Burrel

- — - — - — ✝ - — - — - —

FAITH GIVES HOPE WINGS. HOPE KEEPS DREAMS ALIVE.

To have **FAITH** you Must turn a blind eye to reality, and hope for what your natural eyes do not see. **FAITH** believes that God will do what you asked according to his will.

Yvette Lynn Burrel

ACCEPTANCE

ACCEPTANCE requires patience when it involves matters of the heart. ACCEPTANCE can embrace serenity when we stop wrestling over situations beyond our control. Children and adults have sought acceptance with good intentions from colleagues, peers, and friends. ACCEPTANCE of a love loss can be challenging but will open the door for a new romance. ACCEPTANCE should not be forced; it will come when forgiveness takes the high road. Gaining acceptance into prestigious organizations can promote you to do greater works for humanity. ACCEPTANCE after not getting the job or promotion is only preparation for something better, because I have learned from the experience. ACCEPTANCE is a beautiful thing; it is the gateway to a new journey of hope. ACCEPTANCE clinched is the defining moment that will release wholeness and gratification into my life.

Yvette Lynn Burrel

When you see me,
you are looking at a

Miracle

**It's because of Gods
grace that you cannot
look at me and know
what struggles I've
been through.**

Yvette Lynn Burrel

RESPECT

RESPECT for yourself is not an option, it is necessary and should be taught to maturing adolescents. Every individual is uniquely formed and if they respect others, they too should be accepted and esteemed without discrimination.

1 Peter chapter 2 verse 17
[NLT]
Respect everyone, and love your christian brothers and sisters. Fear God, and respect the king.

Yvette Lynn Burrel

CELEBRATE

Celebrate life,
recovery, wellness,
freedom and family
in this moment because
tomorrow is not
guaranteed; live
for today.

Philippians chapter 4 verses 4 and 5
[[NIV]
[4] Rejoice in the Lord always.
I will say it again; Rejoice!
[5] Let your gentleness be
evident to all. The Lord is near.

Yvette Lynn Burrel

TRUST

TRUST is the foundation that long
lasting relationships personify.
TRUST is earned over time when
reliability maintains self-control.
Your heart can be jubilant when you
are secure in the one you trust.
TRUST that is betrayed creates
skepticism, which causes friendships
and partnerships to dwindle.
Honesty and consistency are qualities
that ensures genuine trust. TRUST is
an innate attribute that every baby
exemplifies with no prior instructions.
Things that destroy trust are lies,
deception, and thievery. When you earn
someone's trust that means that they
have opened their heart to you.
TRUST can not be bought, it will be
evaluated, tested, and finally
established; there is no dollar
amount suitable for trust.

Yvette Lynn Burrel

Philippians chapter 4 verse 13
[KJV]

I **CAN** do all things through **CHRIST** which **STRENGTHENS** me.

I **CAN** have success
I **CAN** obtain wealth
I **CAN** make a change
I **CAN** reach my goals
I **CAN** overcome my past
I **CAN** follow my dreams
I **CAN** have a new beginning

Yvette Lynn Burrel

GRATITUDE

GRATITUDE sends a message straight from the heart to the recipient when thankfulness is openly displayed. Be grateful for what you have at this very moment.

1st Thessalonians chapter 5 verse 18
[NIV]

Give thanks in all circumstances; for this is God's will for you in Christ Jesus.

Yvette Lynn Burrel

MEDITATE

MEDITATE on things
that lift your inner spirit.
Ponder moments of joy.
Indulge your thoughts
towards times that you
were fulfilled. Reminisce
about the good times and
let go of the other.

Philippians chapter 4 verse 8
[KJV]

Finally, brethren, whatsoever
things are true, whatsoever things are
honest, whatsoever things are just,
whatsoever things are pure, whatsoever
things are lovely, whatsoever things
are of good report; if there be any
virtue, and if there be any praise,
think on these things.

Yvette Lynn Burrel

SMILE

SMILE, it does not require currency,
but the effects it will produce to others
is priceless. A smile may be all your
neighbor, friend, co-worker or
family member need to change the
temperature of their day. SMILE
because you are still able to love
and be loved despite any circumstances
at hand. When you transfer a smile to
people you know and those you don't, it
can transform the very atmosphere.
SMILE in the face of adversity because
you know this too will pass. A smile
can generate laughter which will release
endorphins to enrich your livelihood.
A smile given to someone hurting
helps to calm their predicament.
SMILE and watch the bright
sunshine arise within your
relationships and friendships.

Yvette Lynn Burrel

|29

FAITH

Future Expectations

Abiding in assurance

Invokes Gods presence

Thanks God in advance

Hopes until the end

Yvette Lynn Burrel

INSPIRED

Take a moment and think about what or who has INSPIRED your life thus far. Were you INSPIRED by your parents, family, colleagues or friends that gave you support or love unconditionally? Were you INSPIRED by something you conquered in the face of adversity and were able to encourage others that are going through similar circumstances? Maybe you were INSPIRED by someone great, famous, or outstanding that gave back to your community. Being INSPIRED can be contagious in a wholesome way that provokes others to show mercy and kindness. When you are INSPIRED, the world becomes a better place because inspiration cancels depression, hopelessness, bitterness, and hate and releases hope, respect, gratitude and genuine love. Here are a few ways to be INSPIRED, pray, exercise, read God's word and other uplifting books, do something nice for someone in need, hang out with family and friends, and by all means treat yourself to something you enjoy.

Yvette Lynn Burrel

WHAT GOD HAS
FOR YOU IS FOR YOU
AND NOBODY ELSE
CAN HAVE IT NO
MATTER HOW
LONG IT TAKES

II Corinthians chapter 1 verse 20
[NIV]
For no matter how many
Promises God has made,
they are "Yes" in Christ ,
and so through Him the
"Amen" is spoken
by us to the glory of God

Yvette Lynn Burrel

MEMORIES

MEMORIES can prompt us to burst
into laughter when no one else is around.
MEMORIES of our past will continue
to replay in our present as if someone
keeps pushing a rewind button.
MEMORIES of happy times are
cherished moment by moment.
MEMORIES call to mind how we
have matured over the years, which
help us to resolve matters smoothly.
MEMORIES of when we first
fell in love should be rehearsed, and
that will enhance our committed
relationship. We have countless
memories that we hold very dear to
our hearts of relatives & friends
that have transitioned outside of
earth's sphere. MEMORIES of
correction given to adolescents will be
intrinsic when they are getting off
track in life. MEMORIES
are formed everyday, so today start
making beautiful memories that
will last a life time.

Yvette Lynn Burrel

|33

Stay with GOD

Stay POSITIVE

Stay FOCUSED

Stay HOPEFUL

Stay INSPIRED

Stay BLESSED

Stay PRAYERFUL

Stay ENCOURAGED

Yvette Lynn Burrel

— · — · — ✝ — · — · —

FORGIVE

FORGIVE yourself for the mistakes you've made, and allow your past to move out of your present. Forgiving is not forgetting what has occurred, but it is giving you power to move forward. To **FORGIVE** someone means that you will not keep making them apologize for what you have forgiven them for. When you **FORGIVE** it demonstrates strength, never weakness. To **FORGIVE** means you don't replay the event to the person forgiven. When you have been hurt it is not always easy to **FORGIVE**, but it can be accomplished in time. When you learn to **FORGIVE** you will gain freedom. **FORGIVE** because you have been forgiven by our heavenly father.

Yvette Lynn Burrel

DEFEAT IS NOT AN OPTION BECAUSE LOVE CONQUERS ALL OBSTACLES.

Romans chapter 8 verse 37

NAY, IN ALL THESE THINGS WE ARE MORE THAN CONQUERORS THROUGH HIM THAT LOVED US.

Yvette Lynn Burrel

TIME

TIME well spent with loved ones can improve unity, trust, and friendships. TIME has no pity for us as we grow older with each passing day. Mankind lives within the finite measure of time; but there is one who is infinite & dwells outside of time. TIME helps to heal those that are wounded because vitality is renewed every morning. TIME wasted can be an invitation for dilemmas. TIME will divulge if love is authentic or counterfeit. Take time to notice the little things that you have that many others long for, and try to be more appreciative. TIME makes volatile relationships we once endured, a distant and dull memory. Spend your time wisely by saying and doing things that encourage, and transform the populace.

Yvette Lynn Burrel

LORD help me not to DESIRE anyone or anything that is not your perfect will for my life.

Psalm 37 verse 4
[NIV]
Take delight in the LORD, and he will give you the DESIRES of your heart.

Yvette Lynn Burrel

RESTORATION

Whatever has been stolen
whether It was financial, health,
a relationship, children, friendship,
or employment, it will be replaced
with a greater abundance for
your suffering. God's promises
of restoration are true only
if you **BELIEVE** and trust him to
repair the breaches. This can be
a challenge when you have lost
multiple things, but it is attainable
when you exercise the one thing
that really gets God's attention;
unwavering **FAITH**. Instead of
rehearsing what has been stolen
or lost, begin to speak by faith
your expectations and claim them
all with confidence knowing that
God can not lie and will deliver
as his word demonstrates.

Yvette Lynn Burrel

My **H**eavenly Father
He **H**elps me
He **H**ears me
He **H**olds me
He **H**eals me
He **H**onors me
I belong to **H**im

Yvette Lynn Burrel

MY STORY YOUR VIEW

You don't know MY STORY but I have one. You can't see my scars but I have some. You don't know how hard my struggles are, but I have them. You may not see me when I'm crying, but I have shed many tears. You may think I have it all together, but sometimes I'm just trying to make ends meet. You may see me smiling, but it doesn't mean my heart hasn't been broken. You are looking from the outward appearance and that is ok, because YOUR VIEW of me does not make me greater or lesser; it is simply your observation. I am stronger, better, and more focused today than I was yesterday. I am more confident, self aware and courageous today than I've ever been. I choose to live my life happy and free, giving love, receiving love and embracing life. I have MY STORY and everyday I face challenges just like the next person. YOUR VIEW has no entitlement in regards to my success. I choose to stay focused, move forward and leave the past in the past. It's MY STORY and however YOUR VIEW is of me does not take away or add anything to my existence.

Yvette Lynn Burrel

DEAR LORD

Increase my finances, open doors no man can shut and release my wealth that the enemy has been holding back. In Jesus Name Amen.

Yvette Lynn Burrel

WORDS

Your **WORDS** have power and
create a destiny for you when
you speak them. Don't rehearse
negative expressions but rather
articulate your **WORDS** with
anticipation and hope. Speak
positive things into existence
and you will see changes take place.
Faith comes by speaking and hearing
Gods word. You must say and
believe the **WORDS** that you speak
are going to happen. **WORDS**
can build you up even when
you are feeling worn down. The
WORDS spoken from the Almighty
God created the universe. **WORDS**
can impact a person's present and
future state of affairs. Say a kind
word to someone today and watch
them respond with gratitude.
Your **WORDS** have power.

Yvette Lynn Burrel

143

CHOICES

CHOICES are like a blueprint that changes its design with each passing moment. CHOICES change people's lives everyday; sometime for good, and other times end in misfortune. Positive choices can create immeasurable accomplishments in your life. CHOICES demand consequences as an action that must follow every decision. Harmony with humanity negates choices of dishonesty, robbery, and maliciousness. CHOICES to extend yourself to help someone can benefit them and make you feel gratified. CHOICES can result in financial freedom if wisdom articulates louder than squander. CHOICES to read and study will produce higher knowledge and education. CHOICES of discretion mixed with soberness help to bypass unforeseen regret. Make smart choices that will broaden your horizons and brighten your future.

Yvette Lynn Burrel

Chapter Two
The Holy Scriptures
[NLT]
II Timothy chapter 3 verse 16

All Scripture is inspired by
God and is useful to teach us
what is true and to make
us realize what is wrong
in our lives. It corrects us
when we are wrong
and teaches us to do
what is right

For You
Inspired Messages

Y L B

Yvette Lynn Burrel

Isaiah chapter 53 verse 5
[KJV]

But he was wounded
for our transgressions
he was bruised for
our iniquities; the
chastisement of
our peace was
upon him, and
with his stripes
we are healed.

Yvette Lynn Burrel

PSALM 23
[KJV]

A Psalm of David. The LORD is my SHEPHERD, I shall not want. He maketh me to lie down in green pastures; he leadeth me beside the still waters. He restoreth my soul; he leadeth me in the paths of righteousness for his name's sake. Yea though I walk through the valley of the shadow of death, I will fear no evil: for thou art with me; thy rod and thy staff they comfort me. Thou preparest a table before me in the presence of mine enemies: thou anointest my head with oil; my cup runneth over. Surely goodness and mercy shall follow me all the days of my life: and I will dwell in the house of the LORD forever.

Yvette Lynn Burrel

Jeremiah chapter 29 verse 11

[NIV]

For I know the
plans I have for you,
declares the **LORD**,
plans to **PROSPER**
you and not to
harm you, plans to
give you **HOPE**
and a **FUTURE.**

Yvette Lynn Burrel

1 Corinthians chapter 2 verse 9

[KJV]

Eye hath not seen,
nor ear heard,
neither have
entered into the
heart of man, the
things which God
hath prepared for
them that love him.

Yvette Lynn Burrel

John chapter 3 verse 16

[KJV]

For **GOD** so loved the world, that he gave his only begotten Son, that whosoever believeth in him should not perish, but have everlasting life.

Yvette Lynn Burrel

|50

Hebrews chapter 12 verse 2
[KJV]

Looking unto **JESUS** the
author and finisher of
our faith; who for the
joy that was set before
him endured the **CROSS**,
despising the shame,
and is set down at
the right hand of
the throne of **GOD**.

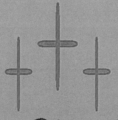

Yvette Lynn Burrel

Nehemiah chapter 8 verse 10
[KJV]

THE JOY OF THE LORD IS MY STRENGTH

Yvette Lynn Burrel

Proverbs chapter 18 verse 10
[KJV]

The name of the LORD is a strong TOWER; the righteous runneth into it, and is safe.

Yvette Lynn Burrel

Isaiah chapter 40 verse 31

[KJV]

But they that WAIT upon the LORD shall RENEW their STRENGTH; they shall mount up with wings as EAGLES; they shall RUN, and not be weary; and they shall WALK, and not faint.

Yvette Lynn Burrel

Romans chapter 8 verse 31
[KJV]

What shall we then say to these things? If GOD be for us, who can be against us?

Yvette Lynn Burrel

Psalm 46 verse 1
[KJV]

God is our refuge and strength, A very present help in trouble.

Yvette Lynn Burrel

Psalm 27 verse 1
[KJV]

A Psalm of David,
The **LORD** is my
LIGHT and my
SALVATION;
Whom shall I fear?
The LORD is the
STRENGTH of my
life; of whom shall
I be afraid?

LORD
LIGHT

Yvette Lynn Burrel

Philippians chapter 4 verse 19
[NIV]

But my God shall supply all your need according to his riches in glory by Christ Jesus.

The LORD will make away Somehow

Yvette Lynn Burrel

Deuteronomy chapter 8 verse 18
[NIV]

But remember the LORD
your God, for it is he
who GIVES you the ability
to produce WEALTH, and
so confirms his covenant,
which he swore to your
ancestors, as it is today.

Proverbs chapter 13 verse 22
[NIV]

A good person leaves an
inheritance for their children's
children, but a sinner's wealth
is stored up for the righteous.

Yvette Lynn Burrel

Psalm 37 verse 25

[NIV]

I was young and now
I am old, yet I have
never seen the
righteous forsaken or
their children
begging bread.

Yvette Lynn Burrel

God cares when your HEART is broken.

Psalm 34 verse 18
[NIV]

The LORD is close
to the brokenhearted and
saves those who
are crushed in spirit.

Yvette Lynn Burrel

- - - ✝ - - -

Psalm 55 verse 22
[ESV]

Cast your burden on the LORD, and he will sustain you; he will never permit the righteous to be moved.

1st Peter chapter 5 verse 7
[KJV]

Casting all your care upon him; for he careth for you

Yvette Lynn Burrel

Romans chapter 8 verse 28
[NIV]

And we know that all things work together for good to them that LOVE GOD, to them who are called according to his PURPOSE.

Yvette Lynn Burrel

Isaiah chapter 41 verse 10
[NIV]

So do not fear, for I am with you; do not be dismayed, for I am your God. I will strengthen you and help you; I will uphold you with my righteous right hand.

Yvette Lynn Burrel

Mark chapter 9 verse 23

[KJV]

JESUS said unto him, if thou canst BELIEVE, all things are possible to him that believeth.

[NIV]

"If you can?" said JESUS. "Everything is possible for one who BELIEVES."

Yvette Lynn Burrel

1 John chapter 4 verse 4
[KJV]

Ye are of God, little children, and have overcome them: because greater is he that is in you, than he that is in the world.

Yvette Lynn Burrel

PRAISE & PRAYER

II Corinthians chapter 10 verse 4
[NIV]

The **weapons** we fight with are not the weapons of the world. On the contrary, they have divine **power** to demolish strongholds.

Yvette Lynn Burrel

For You
Inspired Messages

Y L B

Chapter Three
NAMES OF GOD

Philippians chapter 2 verses 9-11
[KJV]

[9] Wherefore God also hath highly exalted him, and given him a name which is above every name:

[10] That at the name of Jesus every knee should bow, of things in heaven, and things in earth, and things under the earth;

[11] And that every tongue should confess that Jesus Christ is Lord, to the glory of God the Father

For You
Inspired Messages

Y L B

Yvette Lynn Burrel

.

YESHUA

The name of JESUS
in Hebrew that
means SALVATION

Matthew chapter 1 verse 21
[KJV]
**And she shall bring
forth a SON, and thou
shalt call his name
JESUS: for he shall
SAVE his people
from their sins.**

Yvette Lynn Burrel

|70

EL SHADDIA

The ALMIGHTY GOD

Psalm 91 verse 1
[KJV]

He that dwells
In the secret
place of the most
high shall abide
under the shadow
of the Almighty

Yvette Lynn Burrel

71

◆◆◆◆
ELOHIM

The name of GOD the CREATOR and JUDGE of the UNIVERSE

Genesis chapter 1 verse 1
[KJV]

In the beginning [Elohim] GOD created the heavens and the earth

Yvette Lynn Burrel

- - - + - - -

ADONAI

The LORD is MASTER

Deuteronomy chapter 10 verse 17
[NIV]

For the LORD your God is God of gods and Lord of lords, the great God, mighty and awesome, who shows no partiality and accepts no bribes.

Yvette Lynn Burrel

EL ELYON

The Most High GOD

Sovereign ruler of the universe

Genesis chapter 14 verse 20
[NIV]

And praise be to GOD most high, who delivered your enemies into your hand. Then Abram gave him a tenth of everything.

Yvette Lynn Burrel

JEHOVAH
GOD

I AM THAT I AM

Exodus chapter 3 verse 14
[KJV]

And God said unto Moses,
I AM THAT I AM: and he
said, Thus shalt thou say
unto the children of Israel,
I AM hath sent me unto you.

Isaiah chapter 42 verse 8
[ASV]

I am Jehovah, that is my name;
And my glory will I not give
to another, neither my praise
unto graven images.

Yvette Lynn Burrel

JEHOVAH SHAMMAH

The LORD is THERE

Jehovah Shammah is a symbolic name for the earthly Jerusalem and means that God has not abandoned Jerusalem and there will be restoration.

Ezekiel chapter 48 verse 35
[NLT]

"The distance around the entire city will be 6 miles: And from that day the name of the city will be "The LORD is There"

Yvette Lynn Burrel

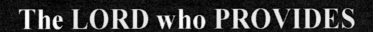

The LORD who PROVIDES

Genesis chapter 22 verse 14
[ASV]

And Abraham called the Name of that place Jehovah-Jireh. As it is said to this day, In the mount of Jehovah it shall be PROVIDED.

JEHOVAH JIREH

Yvette Lynn Burrel

JEHOVAH SABAOTH

The LORD of HOSTS

Isaiah chapter 6 verse 3
[KJV]

[Seraphim Angels cried holy, holy holy]
And one cried unto
another, and said,
Holy, holy, holy, is
The LORD of hosts,
the whole earth is full
of his glory.

Yvette Lynn Burrel

◆ ◆ ◆ ◇ ◆

The LORD our BANNER

Exodus chapter 17 verse 15
[NLT]

Moses built an altar there
and named it Jehovah-Nissi
[which means "the LORD
is my BANNER"].

JEHOVAH
NISSI

Jehovah Nissi the name of
the altar Moses built to
celebrate winning the battle
against the Amalekites.

Yvette Lynn Burrel

The LORD is PEACE

JEHOVAH SHALOM

John chapter 14 verse 27
[NIV]

PEACE I leave with you; my peace I give you. I do not give to you as the world gives. Do not let your hearts be troubled and do not be afraid.

Yvette Lynn Burrel

− − + − −

The LORD who SANCTIFIES
Leviticus chapter 20 verse 8
[KJV]

And ye shall keep my statutes, and do them: I am the LORD which SANCTIFY you.

JEHOVAH M'KADDESH

Yvette Lynn Burrel

The LORD is my SHEPHERD

1 Peter chapter 2 verse 25
[KJV]

For ye were as sheep
going astray; but are now
returned unto the
SHEPHERD and
BISHOP of your souls.

JEHOVAH
RAAH

Yvette Lynn Burrel

JEHOVAH RAPHA

The LORD who HEALS me

[NIV]

Psalm 103 verses 2 & 3

[2] Praise the LORD, my soul and forget not all his benefits. [3] Who forgives all your sins and heals all your diseases.

Yvette Lynn Burrel

JEHOVAH TSIDKENU

The LORD our RIGHTEOUSNESS

II Corinthians chapter 5 verse 21
[NIV]

God made him who had no sin to be sin for us, so that in him we might become the righteousness of God.

Yvette Lynn Burrel

Chapter Four
INCOMMUNICABLE ATTRIBUTES OF GOD

There are both Communicable and
Incommunicable Attributes of
God. The Communicable Attributes of
God include Love, Mercy, Knowledge,
Goodness, and Justice to name a few.
God has given mankind the privilege
of possessing some of his Communicable
Attributes. The Incommunicable Attributes
of God which I chose to include in this
book are possessed by God alone.
Some of them are Omnipotent,
Omniscience and Omnipresent.
You will find more of these
unique attributes as you continue
to read this chapter.

For You
Inspired Messages

Y L B

Yvette Lynn Burrel

OMNIPOTENT

All POWERFUL

GOD is Almighty and
Infinite in Power.

GOD has supreme
power over all that is in
the world and beneath
the earth.

Psalm 36 verse 6
[NLT]

**Your righteousness is like
The mighty mountains,
your justice like the ocean
depths. You care for
people and animals
alike, O LORD.**

Yvette Lynn Burrel

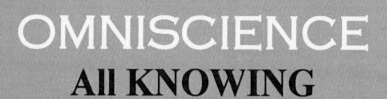

OMNISCIENCE
All KNOWING

GOD knows everything, nothing is hidden from him. GOD does not and cannot learn he knows the beginning and end of all things.

Psalm 147 verse 5
[NIV]

Great is our Lord and mighty in power, his understanding has no limit.

Yvette Lynn Burrel

OMNIPRESENT

ALL PRESENT

GOD is everywhere and **present** at the same time. GOD fills all space and is not constrained by time.

Jeremiah chapter 23 verse 24
[NIV]
Who can hide in secret places so that I cannot see them? declares the LORD. "Do not I fill heaven and earth?" declares the LORD.

Yvette Lynn Burrel

HOLINESS

GOD IS HOLY

GOD has no sin and can not sin because he is HOLY. He sent his son Jesus into the world to die for all sinners. God himself remains blameless, perfect and sinless because he is HOLY.

1 Peter chapter 1 verses 15 & 16
[NIV]

[15] But just as he who called you is holy, so be Holy in all you do; [16] for it is written; Be holy, because I am holy"

Yvette Lynn Burrel

IMMUTABLE

DOES NOT CHANGE

GOD cannot change and
will remain the same
throughout all eternity.

GODS nature, promises,
gifts and perfection
will never change
because he is immutable.

Hebrews chapter 13 verse 8
[NIV]
Jesus Christ is the same
yesterday and today
and forever.

Yvette Lynn Burrel

INFINATE

NO BOUNDARIES NO LIMITS

GOD has no limits as to what he can accomplish. God does not get tired, he does not sleep, he does not learn he knows everything and he has all power.
Isaiah chapter 40 verse 28
[NIV]
Do you not know? Have you not heard? The LORD is the everlasting God, the Creator of the ends of the earth. He will not grow tired or weary, and his understanding no one can fathom.

Yvette Lynn Burrel

SOVEREIGN

SUPREME CONTROLS ALL THINGS

GOD has complete control over
the entire cosmos and reigns as
the highest supreme being.
GOD still gives mankind the
option to choose whom they
will serve. GOD does not
take orders from anyone
and he will do whatever
pleases himself.
Isaiah chapter 46 verse 10
[KJV]
Declaring the end from the
beginning, and from ancient
times the things that are not yet
done, saying, My counsel shall
stand, and I will do all my pleasure.

Yvette Lynn Burrel

SELF-EXISTENCE

NOT CREATED GOD EXISTS

GOD created everything in the universe however GOD alone was not formed. Before time began God existed and after time ends God will still be self-existent.

Hebrews chapter 11 verse 6
[NLT]
And it is impossible to please God without faith. Anyone who wants to come to him must believe that God exists and that he rewards those who sincerely seek him.

Yvette Lynn Burrel

UNIQUENESS

GOD IS NOT LIKE ANY OTHER GOD

There were no other GODS
before him and no other
God can compare to
his Mighty Power.

Isaiah chapter 43 verses 11 – 12
[KJV]

[11] I, even I, am the LORD;
and beside me there is no
Saviour. [12] I have declared,
and have saved, and I have
shewed, when there was
no strange god among you;
therefore ye are my witnesses,
saith the LORD, that I am God.

Yvette Lynn Burrel

SPIRIT

GOD IS A SPIRIT

John chapter 4 verse 24
[KJV]

God is a Spirit; and they that worship him must worship him in spirit and in truth

Ezekiel chapter 36 verse 27
[NIV]

And I will put my Spirit in you and move you to follow my decrees and be careful to keep my laws.

Yvette Lynn Burd

SELF-SUFFICIENCY

GOD IS LIFE WITHIN HIMSELF

The Eternal one does not need
mankind's help with anything.
God is gracious to all people
and allows us to be lead by
his spirit and to be a blessing
to one another. God does
not need water, food or
clothing to subsist because
he is self-sufficient.

John chapter 5 verse 26
[NIV]

For as the Father has life
in himself, so he has
granted the Son also
to have life in himself.

Yvette Lynn Burrel

TRANSCENDENT

GOD IS ABOVE ALL CREATION

GOD is greater and higher than everything that he made.
His attributes, abilities, and characteristics cannot be duplicated or matched by anyone or anything in this world.

Isaiah chapter 55 verses 8-9
[KJV]

[8] For my thoughts are not your thoughts neither are your ways my ways, saith the LORD. [9] For as the heavens are higher than the earth, so are my ways higher than your ways, and my thoughts than your thoughts.

Yvette Lynn Burrel

For You
Inspired Messages

Y L B

FAMIY TRIBUTE WITH LOVE

To my mother, father & 11 siblings
I am honored to be in such an amazing family that
Has been recognized all over the world for the
dedicated service of my two extraordinary parents
in the field of evangelism and ministry. My father
Bishop William L. Burrel is with Jesus and has taken
his rest. He leaves a great legacy for us all to pattern
after. My gorgeous mother Dr. Willi Burrel is an
author and Godly woman that is a role model for women
in multiple states. I have 7 handsome brothers of whom
I am proud to say they all are ministers for Christ
and four of them have been elevated to the office of a
Bishop. I have 4 beautiful, anointed sisters that I am
so grateful for and they are all educated and successful
women of God. We all love the word of God. In the
pages to follow we have listed just one of our
cherished bible passages that keeps us encouraged
taken from the King James Version. We are listed
in our birth order as well. I hope that you will
be inspired by our favorites because they are For You.

For You
Inspired Messages

Y L B

Yvette Lynn Burrel

Family Scripture Favorites I

DAD [RIH]
II Timothy 1:12
For the which cause I also suffer these things:
Nevertheless I am not a shame: for I know whom
I have believed, and am persuaded that he is able
to keep that which I have committed unto
him against that day.

MOM
Isaiah 40;6-7
verse [6] The voice said, Cry. And he said, what
shall I cry? All flesh is grass, and all the goodliness
thereof is as the flower of the field:
verse [7] The grass withereth, the flower fadeth;
because the sprit of the LORD bloweth upon it;
surely the people is grass.

#1 WILLIE [RIH]
Romans 12:2
And be not conformed to the world: but be ye
transformed by the renewing of your mind, that
ye may prove what is that good, and acceptable,
and perfect, will of God.

#2 CARLTON
Psalm 127:1
A Song of degrees for Solomon, Except the
LORD build the house, they labour in vain that
build it: except the LORD keep the city,
the watchman waketh but in vain.

Yvette Lynn Burrel

Family Scripture Favorites II

#3 JUDY
Psalm 117: 1
Oh praise the LORD. All ye nations:
praise him, all ye people.

#4 OZETTA [RIH]
Psalm 91:1
He that dwelleth in the secret place of the
most High shall abide under the shadow
of the Almighty.

#5 AVERY
Ephesians 3:20
Now unto him that is able to do exceeding
abundantly above all that we ask or think,
according to the power that worketh in us.

#6 THURSTON
II Timothy 2:15
Study to shew thyself approved unto God, a
workman that needeth not to be ashamed,
rightly dividing the word of truth.

#7 BEVERLY
Proverbs 3:5
"Trust in the LORD with all your heart;
and lean not unto thine own understanding.

Yvette Lynn Burrel

Family Scripture Favorites III

#8 BRIAN
Psalm 91:1
He that dwelleth in the secret place of the most High shall abide under the shadow of the Almighty.

#9 MICHAEL
Titus 2:11
For the grace of God that bringeth salvation hath appeared to all men.

#10 YVETTE
Psalm 27:1
A Psalm of David. The LORD is my light and my salvation; whom shall I fear? The LORD is the strength of my life; of whom shall I be afraid?

#11 JACKIE
Psalm 37:4
Delight thyself also in the LORD; and he shall give thee the desires of thine heart.

#12 JOSEPH
Isaiah 55:6
"Seek ye the LORD while he may be found, call ye upon him while he is near.

Yvette Lynn Burrel

92791935R00066

Made in the USA
Lexington, KY
09 July 2018